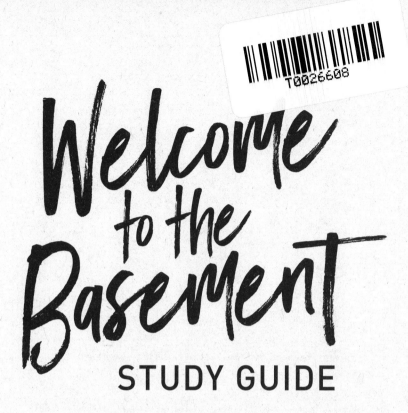

Welcome to the Basement

STUDY GUIDE

A PRACTICAL GUIDE TO BUILDING
JESUS' FIRST-SHALL-BE-LAST,
UPSIDE-DOWN KINGDOM

TIM ROSS

WITH SAM O'NEAL

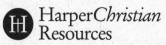

HarperChristian
Resources

Welcome to the Basement Bible Study Guide
© 2024 by Tim Ross

Requests for information should be addressed to:
HarperChristian Resources, 3900 Sparks Dr. SE, Grand Rapids, Michigan 49546

ISBN 978-0-310-17068-6 (softcover)
ISBN 978-0-310-17065-4 (ebook)

HarperChristian Resources titles may be purchased in bulk for church, business, fundraising, or ministry use. For information, please e-mail ResourceSpecialist@ ChurchSource.com.

First Printing January 2024 / Printed in the United States of America

23 24 25 26 27 LBC 5 4 3 2 1

CONTENTS

When [Jesus] noticed how the guests picked the places of
honor at the table, he told them this parable:
"When someone invites you to a wedding feast, do not take
the place of honor, for a person more distinguished than you
may have been invited. If so, the host who invited both of you will
come and say to you, 'Give this person your seat.'
Then, humiliated, you will have to take the least important place.
But when you are invited, take the lowest place, so that
when your host comes, he will say to you, 'Friend, move up
to a better place.' Then you will be honored in the presence of all
the other guests. For all those who exalt themselves will be humbled,
and those who humble themselves will be exalted."

LUKE 14:7-11

A NOTE FROM TIM

The most expensive residential home in the United States is a penthouse in New York City. No surprise there. The Big Apple has always been in a world of its own when it comes to real estate—a world most of us never see. But the details of that particular penthouse are a bit surprising, even for the city that never sleeps.

Located at the top of Central Park Tower, the three-story unit was listed for sale in September 2022 at a price of $250 million. (Isn't it nice when sellers use round numbers? Just makes everything easier.) The unit is the pinnacle of the world's tallest residential building, which makes it the world's tallest residence.

If you were to schedule a showing and take a peek—you know, just in case you've got a quarter of a billion lying around—here is what you would find:

- 17,545 square feet of interior living space;
- seven bedrooms, eight bathrooms, and three powder rooms;
- twenty-seven-foot high ceilings;
- a huge private ballroom that is nearly two thousand square feet by itself;
- a library, a media room, a gaming lounge, a private salon, an observatory, a private gym, and a catering kitchen; and
- the highest outdoor terrace in the world, from which you could observe the curvature of the earth.[1]

Okay, neither of us is likely to be purchasing any New York real estate any time soon. But many people who believe in Jesus and seek to serve Him every day view the successful Christian life as some version of that penthouse at the top of Central Park Tower.

In life, we're taught the only way to be great is to go up. But I want to challenge that idea. I want to show you that the way up is actually *down*. God hasn't called us to get to the "top" where we mix and mingle with the religious elite in our own spiritual penthouse. Rather, He has called us to live our lives closer to earth—in what we could call the "basement."

Think about a basement in the natural sense. Its traditional purpose is for safety. You run to it during a storm—especially a tornado—because it's the safest place in the building. The Bible says Jesus is "the chief cornerstone" (Ephesians 2:20). I don't know about you, but if Jesus is the cornerstone, I want to be as close to the foundation of that building as I can possibly get!

Following after Jesus means rejecting the trappings of the penthouse and instead accepting His call to join Him in the basement. It means taking Jesus at His word when He said, "Truly, I say to you, unless you turn and become like children, you will never enter the kingdom of heaven. Whoever humbles himself like [a] child is the greatest in the kingdom of heaven" (Matthew 18:3-4 ESV). This is the call I want us to explore together in this study.

Let me warn you, moving to the basement in God's kingdom will be *upsetting* and *disturbing*. Those are important words that we will study more deeply in the sessions to come. But suffice it to say, basement-dwellers need to have a lot of stuff shaken up and turned upside down in their lives before they can feel comfortable living down low—and then they get called to do a lot of shaking and a lot of disrupting in the lives of others.

If you're ready to learn more, let's get going. And let me be the first to welcome you to the basement!

— TIM ROSS

HOW TO USE THIS STUDY GUIDE

In this study, you will explore what it means to have Jesus as the "basement" foundation of your life and how that should compel you to "upset the world" to spread His love. Before you begin, note that there are a few ways you can go through this material. You can experience this study with others in a group (such as a Bible study, Sunday school class, or any other small-group gathering), or you may choose to go through the content on your own. Either way, you will maximize your experience by using it alongside the *Welcome to the Basement* book.

The sessions in this study guide are intended to provide you with a basic framework on how you can open your group time together, get the most out of the content, and discuss some key ideas from the book that you are studying together. Each session includes the following:

- **Big Idea:** The opening box lists what chapters to read in *Welcome to the Basement* and provides the key ideas that will be covered in the session.

- **Opening Reading:** A short story or illustration about the topic of the session for you to either read on your own or read through together as a group.

- **Opening Prayer:** A short prompt on how to open your group time in prayer.

- **Beginning Question:** An icebreaker question to get you and your group members thinking about the topic and interacting with each other.

- **Consider Your Life:** A short exercise for you to do on your own to help you reflect on your life as it applies to the topic of the session.

- **Discuss as a Group:** Questions to help you and your group reflect on the material from the book, engage in discussion, and apply the concepts to your lives.

- **Apply What You Learned:** A short personal exercise for you to do on your own after the group discussion time to help you reinforce the key ideas.

- **Pray to Close:** A short prompt on how to close your group time in prayer.

- **Looking Ahead:** A brief note on what will be covered in the next session.

If you are doing this study in a group, you will want to have your own copy of this guide so you can write down your thoughts, responses, reflections, and complete the assessments. You will also want to have your own copy of the *Welcome to the Basement* book to read during the week. Finally, keep these points in mind:

- **Facilitation:** You will want to appoint someone to serve as the group facilitator. This person will be responsible for keeping track of the time during discussions and activities and generally making sure things run smoothly. If you have been chosen for this role, there are some resources in the back of this guide that can help you lead your group through the study.

- **Faithfulness:** Your small group is a place where tremendous growth can happen as you reflect on the Bible, ask questions, and learn what God is doing in each other's lives. Be fully committed and attend each session so you can build trust and rapport with the other members.

- **Friendship:** The goal of any small group is to serve as a place where people share, learn about God, and build friendships. So seek to make your group a safe place. Be honest about your thoughts and feelings . . . but also listen to everyone else's thoughts, feelings, and opinions. Keep anything personal that your group members share in confidence so that you can create a community where people can heal, be challenged, and grow spiritually.

If you are unable to read through the chapters assigned from *Welcome to the Basement* in any given week, still attend the group time. You will get a lot out of listening to the other group members even if you have not done all the reading, and the group members will still benefit from hearing your insights on the questions. Above all, as you go through this study, be listening for what God is saying to you and what He wants you to learn. Be open to hear His words about what it means to be a basement-dweller for Jesus.

Being an Upsetter for Christ

Read chapters 1–5 of *Welcome to the Basement* by Tim Ross.

Big Idea: We spend a lot of time making sure the people in our lives don't feel upset—our family, neighbors, bosses, and others. But if we want to experience everything God desires for our lives, we need to be upset by our Savior.

There are people all over the world who somehow made a commitment to have their lives turned upside down—even me. I came to a revelation that I was not living my life the way I should be. I was determined to make it to the penthouse, but through Scripture and through an understanding of what it means to have a relationship with Jesus Christ, I found out what so many others—to the tune of more than **two and a half billion people** (by most recent records)—have discovered: my life should not be lived the way I want it but the way that He wants me to live it. This threw the way I'd lived my whole life up until that point into chaos and disorder until I landed in the Basement.

— **TIM ROSS** [2]

The USA men's basketball team that went to the 2004 Olympics in Athens, Greece, was supposed to be another iteration of the "Dream Team" that had come onto the stage in 1992. Before that Olympics, professional basketball players were banned from participating in the Games. But a rule change in 1989 meant that players like Michael Jordan, Karl Malone, Magic Johnson, and Larry Bird could all play together on the same team.

The result was a superstar-packed team that defeated their opponents by an average of forty-four points.[3] Now it was time for the 2004 men's team to do the same. They certainly had a dream lineup, with greats such as LeBron James, Dwyane Wade, Tim Duncan, Allen Iverson, and Carmelo Anthony joining the team. They represented the best players in the NBA, which was the best basketball league in the world. So how could they not win?[4]

The short answer is that some of the other teams just played better. The USA team lost its opening game to Puerto Rico, ending a twenty-four game winning streak. They lost to Lithuania. Then they lost to Argentina. Led by Manu Ginóbili and Luis Scola, the Argentines won the semifinal match 89–81 to advance to the finals, where they eventually grabbed the gold.

The day after that loss, everyone in the media was talking about the Argentine squad and their crazy upset. That word was everywhere in the news headlines—"Major Upset!" "Monumental Upset!" "USA Basketball Upset by Argentina!" Basketball fans in the USA were also upset. Up until that point, the USA teams had dominated basketball on the international stage. Everyone expected them to win gold—and win easily.

The upshot was that the world of basketball was turned upside down for weeks after the loss. In fact, one could say the *whole world* of sports was turned upside down. Assumptions were thrown out the window. Expectations were re-evaluated from the ground up. What had once been guaranteed was now upended, and nobody felt confident about what was to come.

It might sound strange, but something similar happens when Jesus enters our lives. He turns over the tables. He upsets the apple cart. He spins our world upside down. It's all for better, to be sure, but the initial experience can still be overwhelming.

Jesus is an upsetter, so to follow after Him means to have your life upset by Him. Not in the sense of being angry or emotionally charged but in the sense of being transformed from the inside out. Up becomes down. Losses become wins. The penthouse becomes the basement. Not only that, but one of our goals in following Jesus is to become more like Him. This means He intends for us to be upsetters too. He expects us to turn the world upside down.

OPENING PRAYER

Heavenly Father, You have a plan for me as I begin this study. You have truths You desire for me to learn, conversations You want me to start, Scripture You have set before me to study, and convictions You have already destined to lay on my heart. In the name of Jesus, I say yes to those plans. I say yes to every blessing and every lesson You have prepared for me in these pages. Thank You for this opportunity to join You in the Basement. In Your name, amen.

BEGINNING QUESTION

If you are engaging this study as part of a group, take a moment to introduce yourselves. Then, get things started by discussing one of the following questions:

- Why did you decide to join this study? What do you hope to learn or experience from it?

  — *or* —

- What has happened recently that turned your life upside down? How did that event change you?

CONSIDER YOUR LIFE

No one stays the same after a genuine encounter with Jesus. The disciples didn't stay the same. Nor the woman at the well. Nor Nicodemus, Jairus, or Paul. When our lives intersect with the Savior of the world, things don't stay the same. They get shaken up, shaken loose, and turned upside down. Take a few moments to consider what your life was like before you encountered Jesus. Then consider how that encounter forever "upset" the person that you used to be.

	Before I met Jesus	After I met Jesus
My biggest goals:		
My biggest fears:		
My view of God:		
My view of myself:		

DISCUSS AS A GROUP

Use the following questions to engage with the main themes from part 1 of *Welcome to the Basement*.

1. We are often told by people that success means continually moving upward—that it means reaching for more, for better, for the best . . . for the "penthouse" suite at the very top. In your own words, what is the difference between reaching for the "penthouse" and living in the "basement" as a follower of Jesus?

2. Our world is filled with definitions of success: money, fame, influence, intelligence, attractiveness, and more. How have you been influenced by these definitions?

3. We are defining the term *upset* in this study guide to mean the following: "(1) to overturn, to destroy the power of, to overthrow, to defeat, or to vanquish; (2) to disturb or derange completely; to put out of order, to throw into disorder." What are some of the biggest ways that Jesus has upset your life in some of these ways?

4. There are three key reasons why you should allow God to upset your life and turn your world upside down. The first is because God is madly in love with you. If you don't live your life from a standpoint of understanding God's love, then you will live it from a standpoint of fear. So . . . how have you experienced God's love in recent weeks?

5. A second reason why you should allow God to upset your life is because His Son sacrificed everything so you could gain everything. He died on the cross so that you could have salvation—forgiveness and eternal life with Him. What do you remember about the first time you heard the message of the gospel? How did you respond?

When Paul and his companions had passed through Amphipolis and Apollonia, they came to Thessalonica, where there was a Jewish synagogue. As was his custom, Paul went into the synagogue, and on three Sabbath days he reasoned with them from the Scriptures, explaining and proving that the Messiah had to suffer and rise from the dead. "This Jesus I am proclaiming to you is the Messiah," he said. Some of the Jews were persuaded and joined Paul and Silas, as did a large number of God-fearing Greeks and quite a few prominent women.

But other Jews were jealous; so they rounded up some bad characters from the marketplace, formed a mob and started a riot in the city. They rushed to Jason's house in search of Paul and Silas in order to bring them out to the crowd. But when they did not find them, they dragged Jason and some other believers before the city officials, shouting: "These men who **have caused trouble all over the world** have now come here, and Jason has welcomed them into his house. They are all defying Caesar's decrees, saying that there is another king, one called Jesus." When they heard this, the crowd and the city officials were thrown into turmoil. Then they made Jason and the others post bond and let them go.

ACTS 17:1–9

6. A third reason why you should allow God to upset your life is because He has a plan for you. When has God changed your plans or adjusted your trajectory in a major way?

7. Read the passage from Acts 17:1–9 on the opposite page. Paul and Silas had not yet "caused trouble all over the world," so these words from the Jews in Thessalonica were both exaggerated and prophetic. What do you think they recognized in the message that Paul and Silas were preaching that caused them to respond in this way?

8. A lot of people believe that God is not using them if they're not preaching from the pulpit or engaged in some other kind of "spiritual" vocation. But God's plans are so profound and strategic that they include people in all kinds of varied industries. What do you feel are some of God's plans for your life right now? (Be specific.)

Let me tell you the good news about the gospel: Jesus didn't wait to see if you **wanted** Him to [die for you]. The good news of the gospel is that before you even knew to ask the question, Christ decided to die for your sins. It's the most upsetting thing that's ever happened in all of human history. Not because it makes anyone angry, but because it presents this amazing opportunity for a shift in a person's life, an invitation to the Basement, all off of a **maybe**.

— TIM ROSS [5]

9. Consider the quote from the *Welcome to the Basement* book on the opposite page. What have you lost by choosing to follow Jesus? What have you gained?

10. In Ephesians 2:10, Paul offers another window into God's plans for us: "For we are God's handiwork, created in Christ Jesus to do good works, which God prepared in advance for us to do." What are some of the main obstacles that hinder or prevent us from living out what God "prepared in advance for us to do"?

APPLY WHAT YOU LEARNED

The "upsetting" experience that we call *salvation* is a game changer. It's a life changer. But when we come to salvation, not everything about our lives changes at once. Receiving the gift of Jesus' righteousness instantly makes us legally righteous in God's eyes, but implementing that righteousness in our everyday actions and attitudes takes a lifetime of growth. Yet here's the good news: God will give us everything we need in order to experience that growth. This is a promise from His Word:

> Grace and peace by yours in abundance through the knowledge of God and of Jesus our Lord. His divine power has given us everything we need for a godly life through our knowledge of him who called us by his own glory and goodness. Through these he has given us his very great and precious promises, so that through them you may participate in the divine nature, having escaped the corruption in the world caused by evil desires.
>
> For this very reason, make every effort to add to your faith goodness; and to goodness, knowledge; and to knowledge, self-control; and to self-control, perseverance; and to perseverance, godliness; and to godliness, mutual affection; and to mutual affection, love. For if you possess these qualities in increasing measure, they will keep you from being ineffective and unproductive in your knowledge of our Lord Jesus Christ.

2 PETER 1:2–8

God provides everything you need to lead a godly life, but you have the responsibility to make use of those gifts that He provides. So, take a moment to evaluate where you currently stand in that process. Use the scales that follow to get a benchmark of your current life and your current level of growth. Specifically, think about where you are experiencing progress in your spiritual life— and where things need another level of upset.

1. To what degree would you say that your prayer life has grown or expanded in recent years?

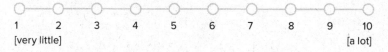

1   2   3   4   5   6   7   8   9   10
[very little]   [a lot]

2. To what degree would you say that your knowledge of the Bible has grown or expanded in recent years?

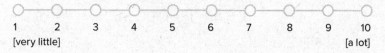

1   2   3   4   5   6   7   8   9   10
[very little]   [a lot]

3. How often do you invite others to join you in the "basement"? (In other words, how often do you share the gospel with others?)

1   2   3   4   5   6   7   8   9   10
[very little]   [a lot]

4. What are some words that describe your experiences with worship at your church? What are some words that describe your experiences with worship at home?

5. What are some habits or strongholds in your life that need to be turned upside down?

PRAY TO CLOSE

Praying for each other is one of the most important things you can do as a community. So use this time wisely by making it more than just a "closing prayer." Be intentional about sharing your prayers, reviewing how God is answering your prayers, and actually praying for each other as a group. Consider this prompt when you do come to a close:

> *Lord Jesus, I have willingly accepted You as the Lord of my life, which means I have given You permission to upset me or turn my plans upside down in whatever ways You choose. When I say, "May Your will be done," I do not mean, "May Your will conform to my will." Instead, may I hear Your voice and obey Your commands each and every day. Please show me today where I need to be upset. Please show me right now where You intend to use me as an upsetter in the lives of others. I say yes to those plans. In Your name, Lord Jesus, amen.*

LOOKING AHEAD

As we move on to session 2, we're going to take a deep look at a word that is both revered and hated: *religion*. This has been true throughout history, and it's true today. What you will see, hopefully beyond a shadow of a doubt, is that religion doesn't work. Especially when it comes to something as important as your eternal destination.

What Upsetters Need To Lose

Read chapters 6–9 of *Welcome to the Basement.*

Big Idea: Religious people are often just that: *religious.* But religion doesn't upset the world; it just makes people angry or confused. Choosing to live as an upsetter for Christ means choosing to let go of religion and instead engage in relationship.

The number one reason religion doesn't work is **the look of it**. Why? Because it doesn't look like Jesus. I'm not talking about the liturgy of the church or a choir robe if that's the tradition you were raised in. It's not about a suit and tie. None of that indicates whether you're operating in a religious spirit. It's the heart behind what you're doing that indicates whether you have a religious spirit or not. Because that's what Jesus is saying in the most scathing way: without the right heart, it doesn't work.

— TIM ROSS[6]

Imagine for a moment that you are on a mission. Let's say, for instance, you are a highly trained special forces operative—like one of those Navy SEALs who conduct small-unit operations in dangerous places all around the world. You have been assigned a mission that seems impossible. You have to sneak your way into enemy territory, neutralize any opposing forces or systems that could uncover you, and rescue a large group of hostages.

What would you do? How would you start? Obviously, you would first need to come up with a plan. You would work out all the details of where you would go, how you would get there, what team members you would choose to accompany you, what particular dangers you would expect to encounter first and how to deal with them, and so on. You would work through whatever clearances were necessary and make sure the path in front of you was as smooth as possible to maximize every chance you had for the mission to be a success.

Then, before you actually took your first step toward your objective, you would need to pack. You would want to sort out your supplies. Grab the right gear. Acquire all the necessary equipment you would need for where you were going. At the same time, it would be important for you to throw out any unnecessary supplies. For example, if your mission involved crawling through a desert, you wouldn't want to weigh yourself down with a frog suit or scuba gear. Such equipment would only serve as dead weight. It would actually hamper you from completing your mission, so you would want to get rid of it. Send it packing.

This is what we're going to think through in this session. The truth of the matter is that you *have* been called out by God and assigned a mission here on earth. Right now in your community— which, by the way, is enemy territory controlled by Satan—there are hostages who need to be set free. There are people in your world who need to have their worlds turned upside down so that they can join with you in God's kingdom.

Once your life has been upset by Jesus, you are called to join Him in His work of upsetting the world. There is some gear you will definitely need to carry in order to achieve that goal. You need to know the Word of God. You may choose to equip yourself with spiritual disciplines and devotional habits. Prayer, which you can view as communicaton with your Commander, will be a must. All of these things are helpful and necessary.

But there will also be some things that you will need to get rid of in order to achieve your mission. There are habits and practices and even ways of thinking that will weigh you down and hamper you if you don't give them the boot. Chief among those unhelpful articles is *religion*, or what we might call *religious thinking*. We will explore all that in this session.

OPENING PRAYER

Heavenly Father, I accept that I am part of Your mission to upset the world, and I affirm that religion will not help me accomplish that mission. Please help me let it go! As I engage with this study, shine a light on any areas of my life where I am doing religious things that are unconnected from You. Shine a light on any of my actions, habits, or thoughts that are dragged down by hypocrisy. Show me what I need to lose in order to join Your mission to upset the world. In Jesus' name, amen.

BEGINNING QUESTION

To get things started, discuss one of these questions as a group:

- What do you like best about the experience of attending church?

  — *or* —

- What is a typical habit in your life that you do every day?

CONSIDER YOUR LIFE

Let's begin with a working definition of *religion*. Religion means going through the motions of worshiping or serving God without actually knowing God. It means lifting yourself up as a religious person when you don't actually know Jesus on a personal level. So, how can you determine the quality of your relationship with God? How can you evaluate whether that relationship is healthy or unhealthy, present or absent, growing or dying? One way is to assess your relationship with God in the same way you would assess other relationships: by measuring how much you invest in them. Take a moment to do that by using the following prompts.

1. To what degree in your life are you investing time in your relationship with God?

1	2	3	4	5	6	7	8	9	10
[very little]									[a lot]

2. In what ways are you investing time in knowing Him?

3. To what degree do you invest your financial resources in God's kingdom?

1	2	3	4	5	6	7	8	9	10
[very little]									[a lot]

4. What does the way you spend your money say about your relationship with God?

5. To what degree does your relationship with God influence your plans for the future?

O—O—O—O—O—O—O—O—O—O

1   2   3   4   5   6   7   8   9   10

[very little]   [a lot]

6. What do your actions and attitudes today—what you have done and what you plan to do—communicate about your relationship with God? Write your thoughts below.

DISCUSS AS A GROUP

Use the following questions to engage with the main themes from part 2 of *Welcome to the Basement*.

1. How would you define "religion" or "religious thinking" in your own words?

2. What are some ways your experiences with Christianity have been influenced by religion in a positive way? How have they been influenced in a negative way?

3. Read through Jesus' criticism of the Pharisees and religious leaders in Matthew 23:13–26, 33–39 on the following pages. How were the Pharisees' religious practices causing harm?

"Woe to you, teachers of the law and Pharisees, you hypocrites! You shut the door of the kingdom of heaven in people's faces. You yourselves do not enter, nor will you let those enter who are trying to.

"Woe to you, teachers of the law and Pharisees, you hypocrites! You travel over land and sea to win a single convert, and when you have succeeded, you make them twice as much a child of hell as you are.

"Woe to you, blind guides! You say, 'If anyone swears by the temple, it means nothing; but anyone who swears by the gold of the temple is bound by that oath.' You blind fools! Which is greater: the gold, or the temple that makes the gold sacred? You also say, 'If anyone swears by the altar, it means nothing; but anyone who swears by the gift on the altar is bound by that oath.' You blind men! Which is greater: the gift, or the altar that makes the gift sacred? Therefore, anyone who swears by the altar swears by it and by everything on it. And anyone who swears by the temple swears by it and by the one who dwells in it. And anyone who swears by heaven swears by God's throne and by the one who sits on it.

"Woe to you, teachers of the law and Pharisees, you hypocrites! You give a tenth of your spices—mint, dill and cumin. But you have neglected the more important matters of the law—justice, mercy and faithfulness. You should have practiced the latter, without neglecting the former. You blind guides! You strain out a gnat but swallow a camel.

"Woe to you, teachers of the law and Pharisees, you hypocrites! You clean the outside of the cup and dish, but inside they are full of greed and self-indulgence. Blind Pharisee! First clean the inside of the cup and dish, and then the outside also will be clean. . . .

"You snakes! You brood of vipers! How will you escape being condemned to hell? Therefore I am sending you prophets and sages and teachers. Some of them you will kill and crucify; others you will flog in your synagogues and pursue from town to town. And so upon you will come all the righteous blood that has been shed on earth, from the blood of righteous Abel to the blood of Zechariah son of Berekiah, whom you murdered between the temple and the altar. Truly I tell you, all this will come on this generation.

"Jerusalem, Jerusalem, you who kill the prophets and stone those sent to you, how often I have longed to gather your children together, as a hen gathers her chicks under her wings, and you were not willing. Look, your house is left to you desolate. For I tell you, you will not see me again until you say, 'Blessed is he who comes in the name of the Lord.'"

MATTHEW 23:13–26, 33–39

4. When have you felt convicted of acting in a hypocritical manner? What steps have you taken to resolve that hypocrisy?

5. Religion doesn't work because it doesn't "look" like Jesus. It doesn't reflect His heart. Use the space below to write down what our culture tends to associate with the "look" of Christianity. In other words, if you were to survey a hundred people and ask them what it means to be a Christian, what would they say?

6. Consider this quote from *Welcome to the Basement*: "If you're walking around and everything you do is just for show, your heart is far from [Jesus]. . . . You're more focused on getting to the penthouse than being in the right place—where He is."[7] How do you respond to this statement? What are some words that you would use to describe your personal connection with Jesus?

7. Religion also doesn't work because it doesn't "sound" like God. Meaning, what religious people say rarely lines up with what God says or values. Where have you seen a disconnect between the values upheld throughout Scripture and the values trumpeted by the church (or by churches)?

8. In Romans 10:9, the apostle Paul makes it clear what conditions are attached to salvation: "If you declare with your mouth, 'Jesus is Lord,' and believe in your heart that God raised him from the dead, you will be saved." What are some other "requirements" for salvation that you have seen added by people in the church?

9. What are some things that you as a Christian do because you feel like they are expected (or even demanded) by others in the church?

If it's the **look of it** that you think will bring you into a special relationship with God, you have severely disconnected yourself from the Christ who came to redeem us from the law. . . . Jesus wants to free everybody from the religious trappings of a to-do list. There is a discipleship process, and there are things that are in place to help you grow as a believer, but if you're really giving your life to Jesus, you will **hunger for and want** those things. You won't need anyone else to create laws to bind you to what they think you should do.

— TIM ROSS [8]

10. Consider the quote from the *Welcome to the Basement* book on the opposite page. In what ways have your desires and appetites changed since you encountered Jesus?

APPLY WHAT YOU LEARNED

In addition to the passage that you read from Matthew 13, there are other places in the Bible where God condemns the religious practices of His people because they were going through the motions of worshiping Him without really knowing Him. For example, long before Jesus' blazing speech to the Pharisees came these words spoken by God through the prophet Isaiah:

> Hear the word of the LORD,
>   you rulers of Sodom;
> listen to the instruction of our God,
>   you people of Gomorrah!
> "The multitude of your sacrifices—
>   what are they to me?" says the LORD.
> "I have more than enough of burnt offerings,
>   of rams and the fat of fattened animals;
> I have no pleasure
>   in the blood of bulls and lambs and goats.
> When you come to appear before me,
>   who has asked this of you,
>   this trampling of my courts?

Stop bringing meaningless offerings!
    Your incense is detestable to me.
New Moons, Sabbaths and convocations—
    I cannot bear your worthless assemblies.
Your New Moon feasts and your appointed festivals
    I hate with all my being.
They have become a burden to me;
    I am weary of bearing them.
When you spread out your hands in prayer,
    I hide my eyes from you;
even when you offer many prayers,
    I am not listening.
Your hands are full of blood!
Wash and make yourselves clean.
    Take your evil deeds out of my sight;
    stop doing wrong.
Learn to do right; seek justice.
    Defend the oppressed.
Take up the cause of the fatherless;
    plead the case of the widow.
"Come now, let us settle the matter,"
    says the LORD.
"Though your sins are like scarlet,
    they shall be as white as snow;
though they are red as crimson,
    they shall be like wool.
If you are willing and obedient,
    you will eat the good things of the land;
but if you resist and rebel,
    you will be devoured by the sword."
    For the mouth of the LORD has spoken.

ISAIAH 1:10–20

God pulled no punches when it came to calling out those who were claiming His name without connecting to His heart. The same goes for us today. Read through Isaiah 1:10–20 one more time. As you do, underline any phrases that are convicting to you. Circle any lines that make you feel hopeful. Then use the prompts below to think more deeply about what you may need to let go of in order to fulfill your role as an upsetter in God's kingdom.

1. What are you currently sacrificing that God never asked you to sacrifice?

2. What rituals are part of your worship practices during the weekend? Which of those rituals are based on looking good or sounding good for the sake of others?

3. What *should* a Christian "look" like and "sound" like? Use the space below to sketch one element of following Jesus that should be evident in what we do and what we say.

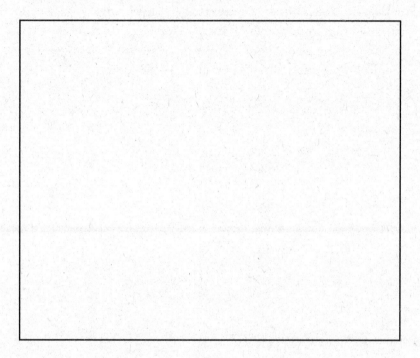

4. Where do you have an opportunity this week to seek justice in your community?

PRAY TO CLOSE

Speak with God about any ways you have noticed religion or religious practices clogging up the wheels of your spiritual life. Consider this prompt when it comes time to close:

> *Heavenly Father, I repent of any hypocrisy in my life. I repent of any actions that have reflected poorly on Your name. I repent of thinking in ways that clash with Your Word and Your values. I repent of any times in which my words did not match my actions. Through Your Holy Spirit, please open my eyes so I can see anything in my life that needs to be released—any aspect of religious thinking that needs to be removed. In Jesus' name, amen.*

LOOKING AHEAD

We've focused for two sessions now on what it means to be an upsetter for Christ. We've seen the need for Jesus to upset our lives, and we've seen the damage religion can cause when we try to look like Jesus or sound like Jesus without really knowing Jesus. As we move on to session 3, we will take a deeper and more practical look at what it means to be an upsetter—what it means to live each day in ways that have the potential to turn the world upside down.

What an Upsetter Looks Like

Read chapters 10–15 of *Welcome to the Basement*.

Big Idea: It's easy to go through our days being upset—feeling angry at what others do or say that we don't like. But upsetters for *Christ* have been turned upside down by the power and transformative work of God so that they can go out and upset others.

An upsetter in the kingdom of God is a person who has been upset by the power and transformative work of God, Jesus Christ, and the Holy Spirit. . . . By definition, upsetters have **five qualities or attributes** that are indigenous to who they are when they come into a relationship with Jesus Christ. If someone is going to lead an upset life and upset others, they have to have these five things. If they don't, then I'm not sure they're upsetting correctly and I'm not sure if anyone they talk to is actually on their way to the Basement. Upsetters must . . . (1) love Jesus, (2) love people, (3) be Spirit-filled, (4) do good, and (5) love life.

— **TIM ROSS** [9]

Let's talk about zombies. (I know—this is a Christian study guide that deals with spiritual topics and spiritual truths, and it seems strange to bring something like zombies into the mix. But work with me for a minute. I'm going somewhere with this.)

Maybe you remember that decade a few years back when zombies were *everywhere*. Not in the real world, thankfully, but in the entertainment industry. For a time, it seemed like Hollywood couldn't make a movie without having zombies in it.

SCRIPTWRITER: Here's the newest script for my cowboy romantic comedy set in Arizona after the Civil War.

PRODUCER: It looks great . . . but how can we get some zombies in there?

There were many different types of zombies in those movies and TV shows. Most were slow and shuffled around instead of walking. But other zombies could be fast . . . like the the horde who chased Brad Pitt everywhere in *World War Z*. Most of the time, zombies were not-so-smart, even to the point of getting stuck by a simple fence. But other zombies could penetrate labyrinths and fortified structures to wind up right where the protagonist was hiding.

Despite those differences, you could still tell every time a zombie came on-screen. No one ever sat on a couch and tapped the person next to them to ask, "Is that a zombie?" When a zombie showed up, you knew it.

There are some similarities when it comes to being upsetters for Christ. For one thing, just like a zombie, you *know* when you encounter an upsetter for God's kingdom. You know when you are speaking with someone whose life has totally been turned upside down by Jesus. Those people look like Jesus, talk like Jesus, and act like Jesus—which means they are radically different from most everyone else in our world. They just stand out.

Also, just like zombies, upsetters for Christ are infectious. (In a good way!) Upsetters don't leave things (or people) as they are. Instead, they "upset" others to help them encounter Jesus. Of course, this then turns their lives upside down as well.

As we work through this session, we're going to take a deeper look at five important characteristics that upsetters for Christ possess. These are the five marks, or symptoms, that are always displayed in people's lives when they've been turned upside down by the transformational nature of God's presence in their lives.

OPENING PRAYER

Heavenly Father, I confess that I have an innate desire for my life to remain as it is. I seem to drift toward what is comfortable and stable—I default to the way I've always done things. I know that applies to my spiritual life and my relationship with You. It's easy for me to settle for routines and patterns rather than the genuine thrill of a loving relationship with You. As I work through this study, please reveal any ways in which I do not line up with Jesus, my Savior.

BEGINNING QUESTION

To get things started, discuss one of these questions as a group:

- What do you like the best about modern love stories? Why?

  — *or* —

- When have you encountered someone you *knew* was a Christian just because of their actions and attitudes? How did you respond?

CONSIDER YOUR LIFE

The first mark of upsetters for Christ is that they are deeply in love with Jesus. They have a genuine relationship with their Savior. Communication is one of the most important aspects of any relationship between people—especially between people who love each other. It is difficult to express that love without regular, meaningful communication. So, use the space below to write a "love letter" to Jesus. Use the prompts below if they are helpful, but make it your goal to express to Jesus how much He means to you and how much He has changed your life.

	Dear Jesus,
The first thing I want to express to You is . . .	
Here is what I remember about the first time I experienced Your love . . .	
Because of You, I know this about myself . . .	
Here is where I most need to experience Your love right now . . .	

So from now on we regard no one from a worldly point of view. Though we once regarded Christ in this way, we do so no longer. Therefore, if anyone is in Christ, the new creation has come: The old has gone, the new is here! All this is from God, who reconciled us to himself through Christ and gave us the ministry of reconciliation: that God was reconciling the world to himself in Christ, not counting people's sins against them. And he has committed to us the message of reconciliation. **We are therefore Christ's ambassadors, as though God were making his appeal through us.** We implore you on Christ's behalf: Be reconciled to God. God made him who had no sin to be sin for us, so that in him we might become the righteousness of God.

2 CORINTHIANS 5:16 – 21

DISCUSS AS A GROUP

Use the following questions to engage with the main themes from part 3 of *Welcome to the Basement*.

1. Think about the way that we are defining "upsetters" for Christ. How have you been that kind of upsetter for Jesus in the past week?

2. Upsetters for Christ possess five important qualities: (1) they love Jesus, (2) they love people, (3) they are Spirit-filled, (4) they do good, and (5) they love life. Which of those five qualities have you most experienced in abundance?

3. First and foremost, upsetters love Jesus. In your own words, how would you describe what it means to love Jesus? What does that look like on a practical level?

4. Read the passage from 2 Corinthians 5:16–21 on the opposite page. What does it mean to live as Christ's ambassadors? What does that look like day in and day out?

"Do not get drunk on wine, which leads to debauchery. Instead, be filled with the Spirit" (Ephesians 5:18). A lot of people have more respect for hard spirits and liquor than they do for the Holy Spirit. But in the same way a drunk person is not in control—and the alcohol makes them do crazy stuff and say crazy things that make no sense—people who are Spirit-filled are also not in control, but **they do amazing stuff and say amazing things** because the Holy Spirit is in control. This is why Paul's comparative analysis is so amusing to me. Because why do that cheap imitation? The Holy Spirit will do the real thing if you'll just let Him. He'll change your behavior. He'll change the way you walk. But you won't be stumbling around. You will walk upright, in a straight line, with integrity, character, and morals.

— TIM ROSS[10]

5. The second quality of people who are upsetters for Christ is that they love people. What do you find easy about loving others? What do you find to be the most difficult?

6. The third quality of an upsetter for Christ is that they are Spirit-filled. Read the quote from the *Welcome to the Basement* book on the opposite page. What does it mean to be filled with the Holy Spirit? How should that influence the way you think and act?

7. What steps are you taking to seek out the guidance and direction of the Holy Spirit in your life? What steps would you *like* to take?

8. The fourth quality of an upsetter for Christ is to do good. This is one that just about everyone can get behind. We all want to do what's right. This being the case, what are some obstacles that hinder or prevent you from doing the good you desire to do?

9. The fifth and final quality of upsetters for Christ is that they love life. Meaning, when we follow the example of Christ, not only are our lives be filled with love but we also love the life we live. What do you love about your life right now?

10. This is what being an upsetter looks like: love Jesus, love people, be Spirit-filled, do good, and love life. In which of those five areas are you currently weak? Why?

APPLY WHAT YOU LEARNED

As we have seen, being an upsetter for Christ means loving people and doing good. Again, most of us are on board with this idea. We don't bat an eye at the concept of loving others—at least, in a generic sense. But we would all be lying if we said there aren't specific individuals in our lives who are just a bit more difficult to love. But the truth of the matter is that Jesus does not let us off the hook that easy when it comes to His command to love others. Look at what He said on this point:

> "You have heard that it was said, 'Love your neighbor and hate your enemy.' But I tell you, love your enemies and pray for those who persecute you, that you may be children of your Father in heaven. He causes his sun to rise on the evil and the good, and sends rain on the righteous and the unrighteous. If you love those who love you, what reward will you get? Are not even the tax collectors doing that? And if you greet only your own people, what are you doing more than others? Do not even pagans do that? Be perfect, therefore, as your heavenly Father is perfect."

MATTHEW 5:43-48

Jesus wants us to love and do good for *all kinds* of people. Even those people we would prefer to just avoid. Actually, being an up-setter means *especially* loving those people with whom we would prefer not to engage. Use the prompts below to think through the implications of this truth when it comes to your life this week.

Who do you interact with regularly whom you disagree with politically?	*What is one step you can take this week to show love to that person?*
Who has been distant or standoffish toward you recently?	*What is one step you can take this week to show love to that person?*
Who has hurt or offended you in recent weeks?	*What is one step you can take this week to show love to that person?*

Whose demeanor makes you feel uncomfortable and even annoyed?	What is one step you can take this week to show love to that person?

PRAY TO CLOSE

Talk with God about the five qualities that upsetters for Jesus demonstrate in their lives. Consider this prompt when it comes time to close:

Jesus, I choose to love You because You are my Savior and my friend. I choose to love people because Your Word says that every person on this earth has been created in God's own image. I choose to be filled with Your Holy Spirit because I am Your temple. I choose to do good because I want to follow Your example and live as You lived. And I choose to love my life because I have been blessed by You beyond anything that I could ask or imagine. Thank You, Lord Jesus. Amen!

LOOKING AHEAD

We started this study by exploring what it means to have our lives "upset" or "turned upside down" by Jesus. As we move on into session 4, we're going to see that the natural outcome of being upset in that way is more powerful than we can imagine. We are called to change the world!

Upsetters Are Disturbing

Read chapters 16–20 of *Welcome to the Basement*.

Big Idea: There will be times when God will use us to upset others' lives in spontaneous ways. But there will also be times when God will call us to *intentionally* disturb those around us—to purposefully shake things up in ways that allow the Holy Spirit to move.

There are all types of moments in Scripture and in the Gospels where people are coming up to Jesus with their issues and begging Him to solve something for them.

"I want You to heal my sick loved one."

"I want You to raise this person from the dead."

"I want You to heal me."

Those were all people that came to Jesus, but I want to show you four instances when Jesus was **the one who initiated contact**. He strategically picked the place, the person, and the piece that He wanted to deal with, and He started upsetting things.

— TIM ROSS [11]

On the afternoon of November 26, 1922, an archaeologist named Howard Carter picked up his hammer, steadied his chisel, and prepared to make history. Carter was on an expedition to the Valley of the Kings in Egypt, and he believed—correctly, as it turned out—that he was standing just outside the lost tomb of King Tutankhamun.

After creating a small hole into a sealed chamber, Carter held up a candle and watched it flicker as ancient air moved from inside to outside. He used a few crude instruments to confirm the air was not poisonous and then peeked his head inside. Here is what he later wrote in his journals about what he witnessed in that moment:

> With the light of an electric torch as well as an additional candle we looked in. Our sensations and astonishment are difficult to describe as the better light revealed to us the marvellous collection of treasures: two strange ebony-black effigies of a King, gold sandalled, bearing staff and mace, loomed out from the cloak of darkness; gilded couches in strange forms, lion-headed, Hathor-headed, and beast infernal; exquisitely painted, inlaid, and ornamental caskets; flowers; alabaster vases, some beautifully executed of lotus and papyrus device; strange black shrines with a gilded monster snake appearing from within. . . . Our sensations were bewildering and full of strange emotion.[12]

The tomb of King Tutankhamun had been undisturbed for more than three thousand years, making it one of the most important archaeological discoveries in history.

For many people, that word *undisturbed* is appealing. Most of us would like that word to describe our lives. Maybe not for thousands of years, but we would love at least a decade with no major changes or upsets in life. Who wouldn't choose to have a few years without disturbances, without interruptions, or without intrusions?

As it turns out, Jesus is one such person. When you read His words and actions in the Gospels, it's clear that He did not leave people undisturbed. He was an upsetter, as we've seen, but He also wasn't content to sit back passively and wait for people to become upset whenever they happened to encounter Him. No, He took an active role in disturbing people's lives.

And He calls us to do the same.

OPENING PRAYER

Heavenly Father, I am grateful for everything You are teaching me through this study. Please help me remember every principle or lesson You desire for me to remember, and if there is anything in these pages or in our discussion that is displeasing to You, or anything that is unnecessary for living as an upsetter in Your kingdom, let it fall away and be forgotten.

BEGINNING QUESTION

To get things started, discuss one of these questions as a group:

- When do you remember feeling thankful that a friend or family member stuck their nose into your business?

— *or* —

- What are some areas of your life that have remained "undisturbed" for a long period of time?

CONSIDER YOUR LIFE

There is no getting around it: being an upsetter for Christ means there will be times when God will call you to actively upset people. Maybe this will be one person at a time, or maybe it will be a group of people. There will be times when God will ask you to step out of your comfort zone and upset the apple cart. Are you ready for those moments? Are you ready to do some disturbing and upsetting in the name of Jesus? Use the following assessments to gain a better sense of where in your life you might need to shore up some courage—or pray for a boost of faith—when it comes to the work that God has called you to achieve.

1. How comfortable do you feel when speaking to others about what you believe to be true?

| 1 | 2 | 3 | 4 | 5 | 6 | 7 | 8 | 9 | 10 |
| [uncomfortable] | | | | | | | | [comfortable] | |

2. How comfortable do you feel about the idea of telling someone that what they believe is wrong or harmful?

| 1 | 2 | 3 | 4 | 5 | 6 | 7 | 8 | 9 | 10 |
| [uncomfortable] | | | | | | | | [comfortable] | |

3. How comfortable do you feel about the idea of speaking honestly with other people about your sins and failures?

| 1 | 2 | 3 | 4 | 5 | 6 | 7 | 8 | 9 | 10 |
| [uncomfortable] | | | | | | | | [comfortable] | |

4. How comfortable do you feel about the idea of highlighting the sins of others or showing them how they have strayed from God's will?

| 1 | 2 | 3 | 4 | 5 | 6 | 7 | 8 | 9 | 10 |
| [uncomfortable] | | | | | | | | [comfortable] | |

5. How comfortable do you feel about the idea of submitting to God in such a way that you say whatever He tells you to say and do whatever He tells you to do?

○——○——○——○——○——○——○——○——○——○
1   2   3   4   5   6   7   8   9   10
[uncomfortable]   [comfortable]

DISCUSS AS A GROUP

Use the following questions to engage with the main themes from part 4 of *Welcome to the Basement.*

1. The closer you get to God, the more He will "disturb the piece" in your life. You read that right. Not disturb the P-E-A-C-E but disturb the P-I-E-C-E. Meaning, the closer you get to God, the more He will upend or uproot those pieces of your life that are not in line with Him. When was the last time that God disturbed you in that way?

2. What is something in your life that you sense God is trying to disturb even now? What paradigms of thought, deeply held beliefs, or habits does He want you to address?

3. Read the passage from John 4:1–10 on the following page. Where do you see Jesus intentionally choosing to disturb the woman at the well and upset her world?

4. Jesus initiated the conversation with the woman at the well because He wanted to offer her an invitation to change (read verses 17–18). In your experience, what "offer" has Jesus given to you lately when it comes to changing your heart and growing spiritually?

5. Notice in the story that Jesus first picked a place to create a disturbance and then picked a person. He identified a person whose life needed to be turned upside down. When has someone taken a special interest in helping you change for the better?

Now Jesus learned that the Pharisees had heard that he was gaining and baptizing more disciples than John—although in fact it was not Jesus who baptized, but his disciples. So he left Judea and went back once more to Galilee.

Now he had to go through Samaria. So he came to a town in Samaria called Sychar, near the plot of ground Jacob had given to his son Joseph. Jacob's well was there, and Jesus, tired as he was from the journey, **sat down by the well**. It was about noon.

When a Samaritan woman came to draw water, Jesus said to her, "Will you give me a drink?" (His disciples had gone into the town to buy food.)

The Samaritan woman said to him, "You are a Jew and I am a Samaritan woman. How can you ask me for a drink?" (For Jews do not associate with Samaritans.)

Jesus answered her, "If you knew the gift of God and who it is that asks you for a drink, you would have asked him and he would have given you living water."

JOHN 4:1–10

6. Prayer is one of the best tools you can use to disturb the lives of others—and it is definitely okay to pray without them even knowing about it. So, what other obstacles get in the way of you spending more time praying for the needs of others?

7. Take a moment to write down the names of some people in your life who need prayer right now—people who need to be upset for the sake of Christ in one way or another. What steps will you take to consistently pray for these people this week?

8. Jesus actively sought out *places* to cause a disturbance, *people* who needed to be disturbed, and then found the *piece* in those people's lives that was out of alignment with God's will for their lives. Where do you see evidence in our world today that people are out of alignment with God's vision and values?

God came walking through the garden of Eden (**the place**) in the cool of the day, looking for Adam and Eve (**the people**), asking "Where are you?" When they respond, "We hid ourselves because we were naked," He doesn't question their hiding; He questions their purpose for hiding: "Who told you that you were naked?" (**the piece**—Genesis 3:11). This is the reality of what it looks like to pick the place, pick the person, and pick the piece. It's having the boldness to push through the bushes, peel away the masks and veils and costumes people are hiding behind, and gently invite them out—nakedness and all.

— TIM ROSS [13]

9. What about the individuals in your life? How can you work with the Holy Spirit (or hear from the Holy Spirit) in order to identify the specific "piece" that needs to be disturbed in the lives of those for whom you are praying?

10. Consider the quote from *Welcome to the Basement* on the opposite page. As you continue to learn to be an upsetter for Christ, what steps will you take to gain or grow the kind of boldness that is necessary for disturbing the lives of others?

APPLY WHAT YOU LEARNED

We have made the claim that upsetters for Christ are *disturbing*. In other words, they fulfill their roles by causing disturbances—and even commotions—in the lives of others. The problem is that for too long, the church has been content to just sit back and wait for people to come to it. "Come join us on Sunday morning!" People do get disturbed for God in church, but we're more likely to impact people for His kingdom if we actively go out into the world and search for those who need His help. Jesus told a parable about that search in the following passage:

> Jesus spoke to them again in parables, saying: "The kingdom of heaven is like a king who prepared a wedding banquet for his son. He sent his servants to those who had been invited to the banquet to tell them to come, but they refused to come.
>
> "Then he sent some more servants and said, 'Tell those who have been invited that I have prepared my dinner: My oxen and fattened cattle have been butchered, and everything is ready. Come to the wedding banquet.'
>
> "But they paid no attention and went off—one to his field, another to his business. The rest seized his servants, mistreated them and killed them. The king was enraged. He sent his army and destroyed those murderers and burned their city.
>
> "Then he said to his servants, 'The wedding banquet is ready, but those I invited did not deserve to come. So go to the street corners and invite to the banquet anyone you find.' So the servants went out into the streets and gathered all the people they could find, the bad as well as the good, and the wedding hall was filled with guests.
>
> **MATTHEW 22:1–10**

If you have spent your life serving inside the banquet hall, maybe God is calling you to step outside. Perhaps He is asking you to go and search for those individuals who need to experience His love. He wants you to take the risk of disturbing those you care about so that He can meet them where they are and turn their lives upside down.

1. Where are some places in your community that there's a good chance you can find people who don't have a healthy relationship with God? List as many as you can.

2. Where does your life intersect with those places? Which of those places are part of your normal routine, and which of those places would you have access to if you chose to go?

3. The king in Jesus' story said, "The wedding banquet is ready, but those I invited did not deserve to come. So go to the street corners and invite to the banquet anyone you find" (verses 8–9). What does this say about God's desire to reach all people with the message of the gospel?

4. The good news is that you don't have to be an upsetter by yourself. When Jesus wanted to turn the world upside down, He formed a team. Who could join you in going to the highways and street corners in order to change lives where you live?

PRAY TO CLOSE

Speak with God about the places you have an opportunity to disturb, the people you know who need Christ, and the pieces of those people's lives that are out of alignment with God. Consider using the following prompt when it comes time to close:

Lord Jesus, I recognize and affirm that the instructions You have given to me in Scripture are commands. They are not suggestions. You have commanded me to "go and make disciples." You have commanded me to be a witness for You in my community, in my city, and in the world. You have commanded me to share the good news of Your life, death, and resurrection. So I say yes to those commands and ask for Your guidance as I go. In Your name, amen.

LOOKING AHEAD

So far in this study guide, we have gained an understanding of what it means to be an upsetter for Christ, what upsetters need to lose, what they should look like, and how they might go about "disturbing the piece." Our final session will be more practical as we seek to put it all together.

Start Upsetting The World Today

Read chapters 21–22 of *Welcome to the Basement*.

Big Idea: We've learned four key principles about living as an upsetter for Christ, and those principles are important and helpful. But at the end of the day, nothing will change until we are ready to get out there and actually turn things upside down.

Did you see all the places where it happened for Jesus? **It all started so naturally.** He's at a well, a woman shows up, He asks for water, a whole conversation breaks out—disturbs her piece—her whole life gets changed, and people get saved. Goes to Peter's house, and Peter's mother-in-law is sick. He goes into the room, prays for the mom—disturbs her piece—Mom gets well. He's walking down the road, and Zacchaeus is in the tree. He goes, "Hey, can I come to your house?" Zacchaeus responds, "Yes!"—disturbs his piece—and Jesus upsets the rejection in his heart. It's kind of organic!

— TIM ROSS [14]

It is no doubt one of the baddest moments in the Bible. If there were TV back in those days, the networks would have called it *Fight Night: Jerusalem*. (Except it didn't happen at night, but you get the point.) It all started when Jesus went to Jerusalem to celebrate the Jewish Passover. He visited the temple there and did not like what He saw. Here is what happened next:

> In the temple courts he found people selling cattle, sheep and doves, and others sitting at tables exchanging money. So he made a whip out of cords, and drove all from the temple courts, both sheep and cattle; he scattered the coins of the money changers and overturned their tables. To those who sold doves he said, "Get these out of here! Stop turning my Father's house into a market!" (John 2:14–16).

Talk about turning things upside down! Jesus saw something happening that was downright wrong. The merchants and money changers were committing highway robbery. Worse, it was highway robbery right in the middle of His Father's house. The entire situation was out of alignment with God's will and God's values, so Jesus did something about it.

Jesus did more than just upset the tables. He did more than just upset the merchants. He upset *everyone* who was participating in and profiting from that system—including the religious leaders, who said to Him, "What sign can you show us to prove your authority to do all this?" (verse 18). It was quite a disturbance!

The disciples Peter and John would follow in Jesus' footsteps when it came to upsetting the religious authorities. One time, they were visiting the temple in Jerusalem and saw a man who was lame from birth at one of the gates. When the man asked for money, Peter replied, "Silver or gold I do not have, but what I do have I give to you. In the name of Jesus Christ of Nazareth, walk" (Acts 3:6). The man jumped to his feet and began to walk.

This caused quite a disturbance, and the people came running to see what had happened. Peter took the opportunity to preach about Jesus to the crowd, which upset the priests and temple guard. They quickly arrested Peter and John and led them away. The next day, the disciples were commanded not to speak or teach at all in the name of Jesus. But to this they replied, "Which is right in God's eyes: to listen to you, or to him? You be the judges! As for us, we cannot help speaking about what we have seen and heard" (4:19–20).

Jesus was an upsetter. Peter and John were upsetters. *You* have been called to be the same. We're not talking here about physical violence but about taking action. We've learned a lot together throughout this study, but learning only goes so far. Sooner or later, we need to *do*. Let's make it sooner. In fact, let's make it today!

OPENING PRAYER

Heavenly Father, You have promised that when I ask for wisdom, You will give it generously to me without finding fault. Standing firm in that promise, please give me the wisdom to be honest with myself this week. Please give me the wisdom to speak openly and honestly as I work through this final session so that I may learn the things You want me to learn—and then do the things You call me to do. In Jesus' name, amen.

BEGINNING QUESTION

To get things started, discuss one of these questions as a group:

- On a scale of one (only a little) to ten (quite a lot), how much do you lean toward procrastination?

  — *or* —

- When have you started a healthy habit that produced good in your life?

CONSIDER YOUR LIFE

We've learned a lot of important truths and principles in this study. But as with anything important, we have to move from learning to doing. So, to prepare for that move, take some time to review your experiences over the past few weeks. In the following pages you will find the four main principles we have covered in the first four sessions of this study. As you review those principles, think of any opportunities you've had in recent weeks to put them into action.

Principle 1: Being a Christian means having your entire world upset (in a good way), and then seeking to upset others in that same way.

When have you recently felt God tugging at something in your life that He wanted to upset?	How did you respond?

Principle 2: Upsetters for Christ need to get rid of religious thinking and religious practices.

What is a ritual or religious habit that's been part of your spiritual life?	Has that ritual been more or less prevalent in recent weeks?

Principle 3: Upsetters for Christ are defined by five qualities: (1) love Jesus, (2) love people, (3) be Spirit-filled, (4) do good, and (5) love life.

Which of those five qualities is strongest in your life?	How have you recently grown in each of those five qualities?

Principle 4: We can carry out the act of upsetting others for Christ by choosing the place, choosing the people, and choosing the piece that's out of alignment with God.

When have you had a specific opportunity to "disturb the piece" of someone who needs it?	How did you respond?

DISCUSS AS A GROUP

Use the following questions to engage with the main themes from part 5 of *Welcome to the Basement*.

1. What is the first thing that comes to mind when you hear the word *sin*? Explain your response.

2. Where do you see the effects of sin in our world today? In what ways have you felt the effects of sin in your own life?

3. The gospel is the ultimate example of upsetting gone right. Jesus came to our *place*, He came for all *people*, and He came to disrupt the *piece* we call sin and its effect on our eternal future. How would you personally summarize the message of the gospel?

In your relationships with one another, have the same mindset as Christ Jesus:

Who, being in very nature God,
did not consider equality with God something to be used to his own advantage;
rather, **he made himself nothing**
by taking the very nature of a servant,
being made in human likeness.
And being found in appearance as a man,
he humbled himself
by becoming obedient to death—
even death on a cross!

Therefore God exalted him to the highest place
and gave him the name that is above
every name,
that at the name of Jesus every knee
should bow,
in heaven and on earth and
under the earth,
and every tongue acknowledge that Jesus
Christ is Lord,
to the glory of God the Father.

PHILIPPIANS 2:5-11

4. Read the passage from Philippians 2:5–11 on the opposite page. Note the opening clause: "In your relationships with one another . . ." What does it look like to engage with other people using the same mindset that Jesus used?

5. Our society does not place a lot of emphasis on humbling ourselves. In fact, humility is often frowned upon and seen as weakness. What would it look like for you to intentionally "humble yourself" at home or at the office?

6. God has called you to be an upsetter for His kingdom, and He expects for you to obey that call. What are some practical steps you can take to search for opportunities to "disturb the piece" of those you encounter each and every day?

Sometimes, I can disturb people's piece the first time I meet them. Other times, it's the ninth time I meet them. Eventually there's an opportunity where the **Holy Spirit** just helps you sense that there's some fear or some intimidation there . . . there's some rejection or instability there. And however He talks to you, in whatever manner you hear His voice or feel the impression of what He wants you to do, you'll hear, "I want you to disturb that." It doesn't matter if you're introverted or extroverted. All you have to do is **ask the Holy Spirit** to give you the boldness to just go tinker with that piece a little bit. Ask if you can pray with them for that. Or follow the Holy Spirit's lead and say something to them that completely blows their mind.

— TIM ROSS [15]

7. Jesus promised His disciples, "You will receive power when the Holy Spirit comes on you" (Acts 1:8). We've mentioned the Holy Spirit several times throughout this study, so let's focus on His work for a moment. What are some of the ways that you have encountered the Holy Spirit's power and His leading in your life?

8. Consider the quote from *Welcome to the Basement* on the opposite page. What steps will you take this week to become more aware of the Holy Spirit's presence in your life? How will you more actively and intentionally listen for His voice?

9. Just like we learned from all those Nike commercials, sooner or later we need to "Just do it." We need to disturb the piece and upset people for the sake of Christ. What is your biggest fear right now when you think about becoming an upsetter for Jesus?

10. As you function as an upsetter for Christ, remember that what you are offering is attractive. The gospel is *good news*, and that starts with you. How has the good news of the gospel not only upset your life but also given you peace and a purpose?

APPLY WHAT YOU LEARNED

The book of James could well be considered one of the most practical books in the New Testament. The author pulls few punches in advising followers of Jesus how they should think, act, and behave in light of God's transforming work in their lives. Just consider the following passage:

> Do not merely listen to the word, and so deceive yourselves. Do what it says. Anyone who listens to the word but does not do what it says is like someone who looks at his face in a mirror and, after looking at himself, goes away and immediately forgets what he looks like. But whoever looks intently into the perfect law that gives freedom, and continues in it—not forgetting what they have heard, but doing it—they will be blessed in what they do.
>
> Those who consider themselves religious and yet do not keep a tight rein on their tongues deceive themselves, and their religion is worthless. Religion that God our Father accepts as pure and faultless is this: to look after orphans and widows in their distress and to keep oneself from being polluted by the world.
>
> **JAMES 1:22–27**

"Do not merely listen to the word." What James is saying is that we can't be content to settle for intellectual assent or understanding. We have to take what we know and put it into practice. This is the "secret sauce" for living as an upsetter for Christ. The *doing*.

Let's go back to the four principles that we've been learning throughout this study. Using the space provided, identify the major obstacles that are currently hindering (or even preventing) you from taking action on each. Then ask the Holy Spirit to help you work out how those obstacles can be overcome.

Principle 1: Being a Christian means having your entire world upset (in a good way), and then seeking to upset others in that same way.

What obstacles are in your way right now?	How will you overcome those obstacles?

Principle 2: Upsetters for Christ need to get rid of religious thinking and religious practices.

What obstacles are in your way right now?	How will you overcome those obstacles?

Principle 3: Upsetters for Christ are defined by five qualities: (1) love Jesus, (2) love people, (3) be Spirit-filled, (4) do good, and (5) love life.

What obstacles are in your way right now?	How will you overcome those obstacles?

Principle 4: We can carry out the act of upsetting others for Christ by choosing the place, choosing the people, and choosing the piece that's out of alignment with God.

What obstacles are in your way right now?	How will you overcome those obstacles?

PRAY TO CLOSE

Pray openly and vulnerably about everything you've learned during this study. Talk as a group about any ways you have felt convicted by God's Spirit. Then consider using the following prompt when it comes time to close:

> *Jesus, I understand You have called me not only to believe in You but also to act like You. You have called me to think as You think and to live as You lived. Please light a fire in me this week to be an upsetter within Your kingdom and for Your kingdom. Give me eyes to see every opportunity You put in front of me to love others by disturbing their piece. In Your name, my Savior, amen.*

LOOKING AHEAD

Jesus said, "Ask and it will be given to you; seek and you will find; knock and the door will be opened to you" (Matthew 7:7). As you conclude this study, remember this instruction to *ask*, *seek*, and *knock*. If you make the effort—even if you have "faith as small as a mustard seed" (17:20)—you can be assured that someone is going to open the door because that person has been waiting for the invitation. You just don't know who it is yet. And remember, you don't have to worry about the outcome. Your role is just to step out in obedience and upset the world for Christ.

LEADER'S GUIDE

Thank you for your willingness to lead a group through this study! What you have chosen to do is valuable and will make a great difference in the lives of others. The *Welcome to the Basement Study Guide* is a five-session study built around the book content and small-group interaction. As the group leader, imagine yourself as the host of a party. Your job is to take care of your guests by managing the details so that when your guests arrive, they can focus on one another and on the interaction around the topic for that session.

Your role as group leader is not to answer all the questions or reteach the content—the book and study guide will do most of that work. Your job is to guide the experience and cultivate your small group into a connected and engaged community. This will make it a place for members to process, question, and reflect—not necessarily receive more instruction. There are several elements in this leader's guide that will help you as you structure your study and reflection time, so follow along and take advantage of each one.

BEFORE YOU BEGIN

Before your first meeting, make sure the group members have a copy of this study guide. Alternatively, you can hand out the study guides at your first meeting and give the members some time to look over the material and ask any preliminary questions. During your first meeting, ask the members to provide their name, cell phone number, and email address so you can keep in touch with them throughout the week.

Generally, the ideal size for a group is eight to ten people, which will ensure that everyone has enough time to participate in discussions. If you have more people, you might want to break up the main group into smaller subgroups. Encourage those who show up at the first meeting to commit to attending the duration of the study, as this will help the group members get to know one another, create stability for the group, and help you know how to best prepare to lead them through the material.

LEADING THE GROUP TIME

Each session begins with an opening reading that either the group members can read on their own or you can read out loud to the group. An opening prayer has also been provided to help you get things started—but feel free to pray for the group members in any way that you feel led by the Lord.

The questions that follow serve as an icebreaker to get the group members thinking about the topic. Some people may want to tell a long story in response to one of these questions, but the goal is to keep the answers brief. Ideally, you want everyone in the group to get a chance to answer, so try to keep the responses to a minute or less. If you have talkative group members, say up front that everyone needs to limit their answer to one minute.

Give the group members a chance to answer, but also tell them to feel free to pass if they wish. With the rest of the study, it's generally not a good idea to have everyone answer every question— a free-flowing discussion is more desirable. But with the opening icebreaker questions, you can go around the circle. Encourage shy people to share, but don't force them.

Following the icebreaker question, give the group members a few minutes (but no more than five to ten) to complete the

"Consider Your Life" exercise. You can then go through each of the ten discussion questions, looking up the passages of Scripture and reading the callouts from *Welcome to the Basement* as directed in the study guide.

After your time of discussion, allow a few more minutes for the group members to go through the "Apply What You Learned" activity to cement the key concepts of the session in their minds. Close with prayer.

PREPARATION FOR EACH SESSION

As the leader, there are a few things that you should do to prepare for each meeting:

- **Read through the session.** This will help you become more familiar with the content and know how to structure the discussion time.

- **Decide which questions you want to discuss.** Based on the length of your group discussions, you may not be able to get through all the questions. So, ahead of time, choose which ones you definitely want to cover.

- **Be familiar with the questions you want to discuss.** When the group meets, you will be watching the clock, so you will want to make sure that you are familiar with the questions you have selected. In this way, you will ensure that you have the material more deeply in your mind than your group members.

- **Pray for your group.** Continue to pray for your group members during the week and ask God to lead them as they study His Word.

Note that in many cases, there will not be a "right" answer to the discussion questions. Answers will vary, especially when group members are sharing their personal experiences.

GROUP DYNAMICS

Leading a group through *Welcome to the Basement* will prove to be highly rewarding both to you and your group members. But you still may encounter challenges along the way! Discussions can get off track. Group members may not be sensitive to the needs and ideas of others. Some might worry they will be expected to talk about matters that make them feel awkward. Others may express comments that result in disagreements. To help ease this strain on you and the group, consider the following ground rules:

- When someone raises a question or comment that is off the main topic, suggest you deal with it another time, or, if you feel led to go in that direction, let the group know you will be spending some time discussing it.

- If someone asks a question that you don't know how to answer, admit it and move on. At your discretion, feel free to invite group members to comment on questions that call for personal experience.

- If you find one or two people are dominating the discussion time, direct a few questions to others. Outside the main group time, ask the more dominating members to help you draw out the quieter ones. Work to make them a part of the solution instead of part of the problem.

- When a disagreement occurs, encourage the group members to process the matter in love. Encourage those on opposite sides to restate what they heard the other side say about the matter, and then invite each side to evaluate if that perception is accurate. Lead the group in examining other scriptures related to the topic, and look for common ground.

When any of these issues arise—or any others not mentioned above—encourage your group members to follow these words from Scripture: "Love one another" (John 13:34); "If it is possible, as far as it depends on you, live at peace with everyone" (Romans 12:18); and "Be quick to listen, slow to speak and slow to become angry" (James 1:19). This will make your group time more rewarding and beneficial for everyone who attends.

Thank you again for taking the time to lead your group! You are making a difference in your group members' lives and having an impact on their understanding of God's kingdom.

SCRIPTURES FOR FURTHER READING

The following are all the passages of Scripture referenced in the *Welcome to the Basement* book. (Key passages referenced in this study guide are indicated in **bold** type.) Take them into your quiet time with the Lord in the weeks ahead and ask God what He wants to say to you through them. Look them up and write them down. Post them around your house so you can see them often. You *can* hear the voice of the Holy Spirit. All you have to do is get to know Him.

SESSION 1: BEING AN UPSETTER FOR CHRIST

Acts 17:1–9	(chapter 2)
John 3:16	(chapter 3)
Ephesians 1:4–5	(chapter 3)
Romans 8:28–30	(chapter 3)
Romans 5:6–8	(chapter 4)
Jeremiah 29:11	(chapter 5)
Ephesians 2:10	(chapter 5)
Psalm 18:32	(chapter 5)
Psalm 139:14	(chapter 5)
Romans 8:37–39	(chapter 5)
1 Corinthians 3:16	(chapter 5)

2 Corinthians 5:12	(chapter 5)
2 Corinthians 5:20	(chapter 5)
1 Thessalonians 1:4	(chapter 5)
2 Timothy 1:7	(chapter 5)
1 John 3:1	(chapter 5)
2 Peter 1:3–8	(study guide)

SESSION 2: WHAT UPSETTERS NEED TO LOSE

Amos 5:18–27	(chapter 6)
Matthew 23:1–26	(chapter 6)
Acts 19:13–22	(chapter 7)
Philippians 2:3–11	(chapter 7)
Matthew 11:28–30	(chapter 8)
Romans 10:9	(chapter 8)
Matthew 5:17–20	(chapter 9)
Isaiah 1:2–20	(chapter 9)

SESSION 3: WHAT AN UPSETTER LOOKS LIKE

Ephesians 6:23–24	(chapter 11)
Matthew 5:43–48	(chapter 12)
Ephesians 5:18	(chapter 13)
Romans 8:11	(chapter 13)
Acts 10:38	(chapter 14)
John 14:15–18	(chapter 14)
John 2:1–11	(chapter 14)
Matthew 14:13–21	(chapter 14)
Mark 6:32–44	(chapter 14)
Luke 9:10–17	(chapter 14)
John 6:1–14	(chapter 14)
Luke 19:1–10	(chapter 14)
Ephesians 5:2	(chapter 14)
Nehemiah 8:10	(chapter 14)
2 Corinthians 5:16–21	(study guide)

SESSION 4: UPSETTERS ARE DISTURBING

Matthew 7:3	(chapter 16)
John 4:1–30	(chapter 17)
Matthew 8:14–15	(chapter 18)
Leviticus 24:19–21	(chapter 19)
Matthew 22:1–14	(chapter 20)
Luke 14:15–24	(chapter 20)
Genesis 3:11	(chapter 20)

SESSION 5: START UPSETTING THE WORLD TODAY

Luke 23:33–46	(chapter 21)
Philippians 2:5–11	(chapter 21)
John 2:14–16, 18	(study guide)
Acts 3:6, 19–20	(study guide)
Acts 1:8	(study guide)
James 1: 22–27	(study guide)
Matthew 7:7	(study guide)
Matthew 17:20	(study guide)

NOTES

1. Sarah Jackson, "Take a Look Inside the Most Expensive Home in the Country, a Penthouse in New York City's Central Park Tower That Is Listed for $250 Million," Insider, May 2, 2023, https://www.businessinsider.com/most-expensive-home-250-million-nyc-penthouse-central-park-tower-2022-9.
2. Tim Ross, *Welcome to the Basement* (Nashville: Nelson Books, 2024), 14.
3. "1992 United States Men's Olympic Basketball Team," Wikipedia.com, https://en.wikipedia.org/wiki/1992_United_States_men%27s_Olympic_basketball_team.
4. "2004 United States Men's Olympic Basketball Team," Wikipedia.com, https://en.wikipedia.org/wiki/2004_United_States_men%27s_Olympic_basketball_team.
5. Ross, *Welcome to the Basement*, 36.
6. Ross, *Welcome to the Basement*, 51–52.
7. Ross, *Welcome to the Basement*, 62.
8. Ross, *Welcome to the Basement*, 65, 79.
9. Ross, *Welcome to the Basement*, 101, 103.
10. Ross, *Welcome to the Basement*, 127, 129.
11. Ross, *Welcome to the Basement*, 158–159.
12. Howard Carter, "Tutankhamun: Anatomy of an Excavation, Howard Carter's Diaries and Journals," Griffith Institute, Oxford, October 6, 2010, http://www.griffith.ox.ac.uk/gri/4sea1not.html.
13. Ross, *Welcome to the Basement*, 191–192.
14. Ross, *Welcome to the Basement*, 214.
15. Ross, *Welcome to the Basement*, 212.

ABOUT THE AUTHOR

Tim Ross gave his life to Jesus on January 14, 1996, and preached his first sermon on February 25, 1996. For nearly thirty years he has preached around the world and served the local church in several ministry capacities, including youth evangelist, young adult pastor, director of student ministries, associate campus pastor, executive pastor of apostolic ministries, and lead pastor. Tim now spends his time as a podcaster (of *The Basement with Tim Ross*), influencer, author, consultant, and speaker. Tim has been married to Juliette since 1999 and they have two sons, Nathan and Noah. For more information about Tim, visit upsettheworld.com and follow him on Instagram at @upsetthegram.

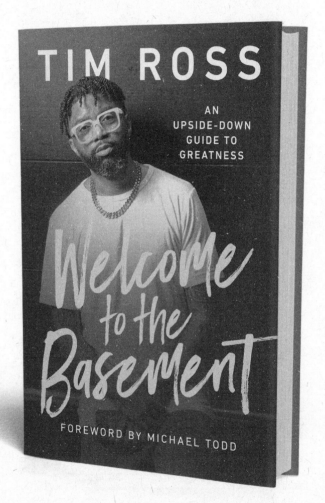